KODIAK KINGS

KODIAK  KINGS

JASON WOOD

INTRODUCTION BY LARRY VAN DAELE

NODIN PRESS

Introduction by Larry Van Daele
Text by Jason Wood
Photos by Jason Wood
Designed by Sarah Ward Rathe

Printed and bound in China by Everbest Printing Co. Ltd.

10 9 8 7 6 5 4 3 2 1

ISBN 1-932472-44-4

Nodin Press
530 N. Third Street
Suite 120
Minneapolis, MN 55401

TO MY WIFE, RENEÉ

Your love, encouragement, and never-ending support

are the reasons this book was possible.

Thank you and God bless you.

CONTENTS

This boar stares me down and juts out his lower lip while passing by on the riverbank.

This map is an original art rendition by Bruce W. Nelson for the Kodiak Island Convention & Visitors Bureau and is printed with their permission.

INTRODUCTION

THERE SEEMS TO BE A SPECIAL RELATIONSHIP BETWEEN PEOPLE AND BEARS.

At one extreme, we fear them as unpredictable demons endangering our lives and those of our children. They are vilified as disparaging predators that cannot be tolerated near livestock or homes because they kill and destroy with heartless cruelty. On the other end of the emotional spectrum, bears are seen as cuddly, bumbling friends. They share our children's lives and imaginations as stuffed animals, cartoons, and bedtime stories. We extend that love and allure into our adulthood as we watch television shows about them, marvel at them at zoos, and, for the more ambitious souls, venture into their natural habitats to meet them in person.

As you peruse the beautiful images in this book, there will be a temptation to rely on your old stereotypes about bears. It is unavoidable to breeze through and emotionally categorize each photo as "cute," "funny," "scary," or some other categorization of your feelings. Undoubtedly there will also be a number of pages that really catch your eye and keep you for a few minutes as you raise them to the higher level of "beautiful" or "fascinating."

But the truly beautiful thing about these pictures is the glimpse they give us into the mysterious and magnificent lives of Kodiak bears. If you want to step away

from the tendency to "humanize" bears, you have to take a little time to better understand how they perceive the world and interact with it.

The general life history of Kodiak bears has been the subject of speculation and study ever since humans first arrived on Kodiak island and its archipelago, which stretches nearly 177 miles. Alutiiq Natives have had a special relationship with the island's bears, treating them as sacred brethren as well as sources of food and hides. Hunters and residents had a keen interest in learning as much as possible about the bears so they could live with them and pursue them as safely and efficiently as possible. The first scientific investigations were collecting trips to document the size of Kodiak bears in the late

1800s. During the early part of the 20th century, research was focused on bear predation on salmon and cattle. As the value of bears as a trophy animal for hunters increased in the 1950s, research emphasis shifted to investigations of baseline information on what bears do and need during their lives. Biologists refined methods of capturing and marking bears and began incorporating radio telemetry. This has allowed a more in-depth and objective window into the secrets of individual bears and better ways to estimate population parameters like productivity, survival and density.

From the time a cub emerges from her mother's womb, hairless, blind, and totally vulnerable, a bear's perception of the world is different from ours. She begins her life in the dark, sharing the security of the den with her mother and siblings. While winter storms ravage the mountainside where their den has been dug, her mother provides warmth and sustenance. At the time she is born in February, she weighs less than a pound, and she typically shares her new life with two littermates. Because of the unconventional reproductive process exhibited by bears, called delayed implantation, each of the cubs may or may not be from the same father. At first they spend most of their time suckling, but within a couple months they are actively exploring the cramped space of the den and interacting with siblings even though their mother sleeps most of the time. When they finally emerge from the den in June, the cubs weigh about 15 pounds and are feisty and curious.

In spite of being without food and water for over six months, mothers of new cubs often take them to even higher and more remote areas for the first month after emerging from their den. The reason for this seemingly odd behavior is to protect them from adult male bears, which are known to prey upon new cubs. Scientists have speculated on the reasons for such cannibalistic behavior without coming to any completely accepted conclusion. One likely reason is that soon after mother bears lose their cubs they again become receptive to courting males. When they have cubs, however, they are not only physiologically incapable of reproducing, they also have notoriously strong maternal instincts and no tolerance whatsoever for males or anything else that potentially threatens their offspring.

As spring progresses into early summer, the families get serious about the tasks of eating and learning. They move down into lower terrain amongst the other bears. Roots and rapidly developing grasses and forbs are the preferred diet for mom. Her digestive system is not specifically adapted for breaking down vegetative matter, so she has to make up for the deficiency by eating large quantities, and restricting her diet to plants that are more easily processed. Her cubs, on the other hand, are content with the warm milk that is produced from her rations. As mom lies on her back, the new cubs clamor onto her stomach and chest and utter a purring sound as they suckle and eventually fall asleep. Bears are naturally crepuscular, sleeping mid-day and night, with the greatest activity near dawn and dusk. When faced with competition for food or space, they adopt a more nocturnal lifestyle.

But sleep usually does not last long – there is too much to do. Bears are intelligent animals, probably ranking somewhere between dogs and primates. Cubs learn about life from their mothers and from their own experiences. Like all intelligent animals, they have individual personalities, and even as young cubs it is evident that they are not unthinking clones.

Bears also have acute senses to perceive their surroundings. Their eyesight is about as keen as ours, but they do not rely on that sense the way we do – it is supplemental to their other senses. A bear's hearing is about as good as a dog's, which is not spectacular compared to some other animals, but is still better than ours. The sense bears rely on most is their sense of smell. A bear's olfactory acuity is extraordinary – perhaps four to five times better than a dog's and immeasurably better than ours. They trust this sense more than any other to identify each other, to warn them of opportunity and danger, and to help them decipher the world around them. In essence they can probably "see" smells as they waif and eddy on the wind and around terrain.

For the next two to three years, the cubs will stay with their mother following a seasonal round of gathering foods and denning. Though Kodiak bears are often touted as the world's largest carnivore, they are really omnivores. They typically spend more time eating grass, plants and berries than meat. In some areas, kelp that has washed up on the beach, and the myriad small decomposing organisms within it, make up a large part of bears' diets. Fish are an important part of the diet of most, but not all, Kodiak bears. Some bears also kill and eat deer and elk, but in most cases they do not expend the time or effort necessary to chase and kill mammals. Their favorite mammalian food item is undoubtedly the dead whales that periodically wash ashore. Not only do these bounties from the sea provide copious amounts of fat and protein, they also supply a source of unparalleled odor. It seems odd that an animal with such a refined sense of smell would derive such unbridled satisfaction from rolling in the stench of a decaying whale.

Bears use the most nutritious parts of their food to maximize their weight gain. Grass and forbs are only used while they are rapidly growing in the spring and early summer. Brains, flesh and eggs are preferred parts of the salmon. Internal organs of deer, elk and cattle are eaten first when one is killed or scavenged. Berries are used most often when they are ripe and sugars are at their highest level.

During most of the year, bears stay either alone or in their immediate family groups. When summer brings the spawning salmon back to the archipelago, cubs must learn new social skills as these concentrated food sources attract other bears. Eons of education have honed these skills so that encounters are often subtle and succinct, and the cubs learn by observing and by the occasional well-placed cuff from an impatient mother. The bears have developed a complex language and social structure to express their feelings and avoid fights. Even at times when tempers flare between adult bears, there are still strict rules of etiquette and serious injuries are rare.

Bears on Kodiak begin entering their dens in late October. Almost all dens are dug in areas that are well drained – there are few caves or natural cavities available on the islands. Most bears return to the same area to den, although individual dens usually collapse during the summer, so excavation is necessary each year. Pregnant sows are usually the first to go to dens and males are the last. Males begin emerging from their dens in early April, while sows with new cubs may stay in dens until late June. Some males may forego denning altogether, staying awake all winter.

A young cub discovers a new and harsh world when she comes out of the den as a three-year-old. She is about as big as her mom and her brother is even bigger. But, just as they are preparing for another exciting year of discovering food and adventure, mom's attitude changes dramatically. She is no longer tolerant of their antics, and eventually goes so far as to become aggressive towards them. This family breakup is often a heart-rending time, with the cubs completely bewildered by their mother's dramatic mood swing. This "tough-love" is necessary, however, as mom prepares to start a new family – accepting the advances of the males she so diligently kept at bay for the past few years.

The next couple of years are especially dangerous for the cubs that have now graduated to become teenagers of the bear world. Besides the obvious dangers of having to fend for themselves to find food and test their social skills, some of them share an attitude with other "teenage" animals, and they do not have a firm grasp of the dangers of risky behaviors. Many will take dangerous chances or push into situations with people or other bears that can be comical or even deadly.

Those that survive this transition into adulthood have the capability to start families of their own when they are about five to seven years old, but most do not successfully produce cubs until they are seven to nine years old. Females can continue to produce cubs throughout their lives. The average interval between litters is about four years, and about half of the cubs that are born survive to adulthood. Mating season is during May and June. They are serially monogamous (having one partner at a time), staying together for a couple days or a couple weeks. As soon as the egg is fertilized and divides a few times, it enters a state of suspended animation until autumn when it finally implants on the uterine wall and begins to grow again.

Kodiak bears are a closed population. We suspect that there has been little or no genetic exchange with bears on the mainland of Alaska for about 12,000 years, yet there is no evidence that their lack of genetic diversity has hampered the population. Even though the archipelago is isolated and relatively small, it offers a wide variety of habitats and resources for bears. Kodiak bears are adaptable and intelligent, giving them individual personalities, habitat use patterns, and habits. There are no natural physical or man-made barriers to bear movement across the island. It would be physically possible for a bear to traverse the entire length of the island in less than a week, but few bears make such forays. They do not defend territories, but they do have

EVEN THOUGH THE ARCHIPELAGO IS ISOLATED AND RELATIVELY SMALL, IT OFFERS A WIDE VARIETY OF HABITATS AND RESOURCES FOR BEARS.

traditional home range areas that they use each year. Because of the rich variety of foods available on Kodiak, bears here have some of the smallest home ranges of any brown bear population in the world.

Females usually stay within the same area in which they were raised. Males go further afield, and perhaps this is nature's way of assuring genetic diversity on an island with rich resources and densely populated bears. When fully grown these males can reach weights of 1,500 lbs (700 kg) and lengths of over 11 ft (3.5 m) – another testament to the unsurpassed quality of the habitat in which they reside. Kodiak bears can live for over 30 years in this wild land.

Fortunately, the bear population and habitat on the Kodiak archipelago are currently healthy. Over two-thirds of Kodiak Island is included in the Kodiak National Wildlife Refuge, and habitat within the refuge is protected. Kodiak's inland habitat is contiguous and intact. Coastal areas have much greater human activity, but it is generally restricted to isolated areas and small numbers of people. Roads are restricted to the northeast coast of the island, and the immediate vicinity of villages. Salmon management for sustained yield is a high priority on the archipelago, and bear predation is factored in to escapement goals. The only large-scale disruption of inland habitat, the Terror Lake hydroelectric project, was completed in 1985 with minimal direct or indirect adverse impact to bears or their habitat due to a conscious effort to work with and around the bears.

Afognak Island has experienced considerable habitat alteration in the past 25 years due to commercial logging. Although there have been no objective studies, we suspect that these activities have not had major adverse impacts on the bear

population because of continued healthy salmon runs, good berry and grass production, little direct persecution and limited general access to logging roads.

Research indicates that there are probably as many bears now (about 3,000) as there have ever been in history. A restricted hunt allows hunters to kill a limited number of bears each year under a closely monitored program. We estimate that in 2004, hunters spent an approximately $4.5 million on Kodiak bear hunts. High economic value of bear hunting results in a demand for as many bear hunts as possible, so the bear population status and hunter harvests are closely scrutinized and micro-managed by the Alaska Department of Fish and Game and the U.S. Fish and Wildlife Service.

Public interest in watching brown bears has increased dramatically on Kodiak during the past 15 years. Some of this activity is incidental to other pursuits such as sport fishing, hiking, or flight seeing, but much of it is specifically targeted at bear viewing. Whenever bears and people interact with each other there are potential benefits and dangers for both species. Wildlife managers work in close concert with fishermen and bear-viewers to minimize adverse impacts on bears and their habitat while maximizing the opportunity for people to learn about and enjoy bears. There is also an ongoing effort to balance the biological and ethical concerns of allowing bear hunting and bear viewing in the same areas.

The people of Kodiak have proven their desire and ability to continue to coexist with bears. About 14,000 people that call the islands home, and most have learned how to live with bears both in their backyards as well as in the backcountry. We are also anxious to share our knowledge with the thousands of visitors that come each year to fish, hunt, hike and watch bears. The end result has been a healthy respect of the bears and a commitment to protect bear habitat. Although bear/human encounters are common, only one person has been killed by a bear on Kodiak in the past 75 years, and only about once every two years does a bear injure a person.

I sincerely hope you enjoy this book and use it as your primer into the world of the Kodiak bear. In the end, I also hope that it will inspire you to look beyond the superficial beauty of the photos and catch a hint of the spirit of these extraordinary denizens of our special islands.

LARRY VAN DAELE
WILDLIFE BIOLOGIST

ALASKA DEPARTMENT OF FISH AND GAME
KODIAK

THE
PHOTOGRAPHS

A golden colored sow, or female bear, snatches
a dark red sockeye salmon from the river.

This juvenile bear walks off into the sunset.

These two juvenile bears find themselves wrestling in a field of fireweed.

The ecosystem that supports these bears on Kodiak Island is not only healthy but stunningly beautiful as well.

This big boar, or male bear, burst through the brush and forced all the other fishing bears to yield the best fishing spots to him.

A yearling cub stays close to mama hoping to get some scraps to eat.

A huge boar appears at the river mouth and surveys the situation
before taking over the prime fishing areas.

Even after mom kicks them out, the sibling rivalry continues at the river.

This juvenile bear peers over the edge to get a better view of the ADFG salmon counting weir.

This sow lost most of her right ear in a fight and is looking very lean and dangerous. She has been unable to catch much food for her cubs or herself. I photographed her one month later, when she had healed and was able to fish quite well.

Sibling rivalry starts early as these cubs learn how to live in their world.

Some cubs develop a distinct collar of light colored fur around their neck, like this yearling.

A mature bald eagle sits on a tree branch and waits for its mate to return. Eagles are a big part of the Kodiak ecosystem

As the sun sets behind this old sow, she wades the shallows of a
river looking for dinner.

Young sibling cubs play wrestle and learn valuable skills they will
need later in life.

Surprised, I turned around and saw this sow moving around
behind me to get to the river.

This two-year-old cub munches on a little grass as he leaves
the fishing area.

It is always fun to watch yearling cubs fight and tread water at the same time.

A lone bear eats a fresh caught sockeye while other salmon leap through the air in their struggle to get up stream

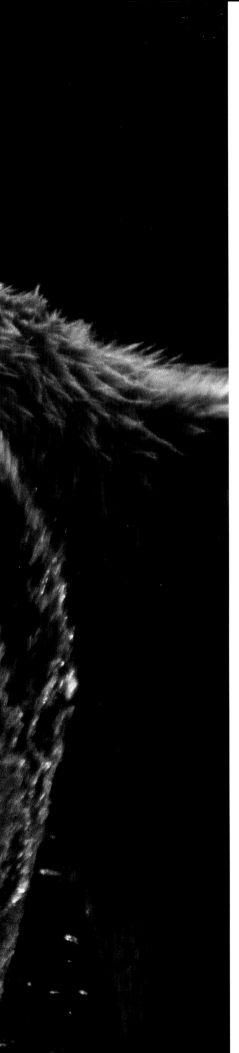

Two juvenile bears wrestle near an Alaska Dept. of Fish and Game salmon counting weir.

This bear stops for a quick rest as he climbs up a steep riverbank.

Using her claws like hands, this sow tears a fresh sockeye salmon apart.

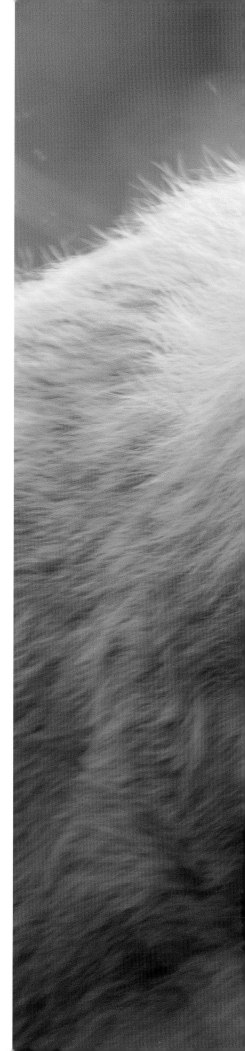

This beautiful blonde sow tolerates the many insects that buzz around her.

Two bears saunter down to the beach as the fog rolls in behind them.

These red fox pups are just learning to find scraps of food along the beach on their own.

This sow teaches her yearling cub many survival skills while at the river

This juvenile bear grabs a lazy nap after fishing all morning.

This bear keeps a close eye on me as he eats the old king salmon
carcass he dug off the river bottom.

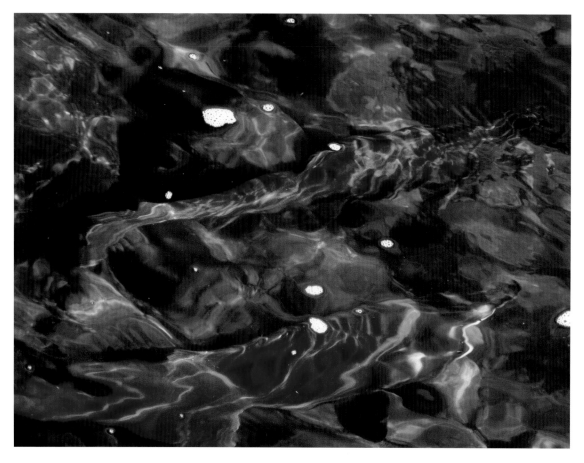

These mature sockeye salmon have made it back to their
spawning grounds to breed and feed the entire ecosystem.

This old sow has perfected the skills needed to catch and hold
salmon with her claws while she leisurely eats.

This juvenile bear carries off a dark pink salmon he just caught.

A protective sow keeps a wary eye on me as she fishes with her cubs.

These two bears stand up in a field of fireweed to try to better detect my scent.

This mature sow got lazy and grabbed one of the slower moving post-spawn sockeye salmon

A sow appears at sunset with her three cubs in tow.

A mother bear is the ultimate protector of her helpless cubs.

Knowing there are other bears around, this sow keeps her cubs
close while approaching the river.

A lone sow walks her cubs through the beauty that is Kodiak.

This two-year-old cub literally waits in the weeds until mama catches a fish, and then he races to her side.

Two cubs wrestle while treading water at the mouth of a river.

This sow catches a short nap after fishing to feed herself and her three yearling cubs.

This sow stares me down as she enters the river with her cubs following behind.

A cub sniffs at mom as they share a meal of pink salmon.

An immature bald eagle soars above the river just before sunrise.

After dragging her salmon onto the bank to eat this sow looks back to make sure she knows where I am while eating

After wrestling with each other, the cub in front returns to mama with a gash across his nose.

This bear mugs for the camera as I photograph him along a hillside.

Some bears prefer to carry their freshly caught salmon out of the
river to eat in peace on the bank.

For bears, eating involves lots of pulling and tearing with both teeth and claws.

Fishing at sunset, this boar prefers to wait and let the fish come to him.

his tired sow is ready for a nap after nursing her yearling cubs.

This boar's preferred fishing method was to literally chase the fish down. His size is a testament to his speed and skill.

These really white and worn claws are sure signs of an old bear.

I was amazed that this sow leaned back and allowed her cubs to nurse while I was photographing them from only 40 feet away.

In between salmon runs this bear has learned to dig in the mud at the river bottom to find old King salmon carcasses that are washing back to sea.

This bear shakes his mane as he swims in the tidal river mouth.

young cub with a beautiful collar pauses to
watch me photograph him.

Kodiak bear cubs don't take direction very well.

This yearling cub leads the family to the river while a juvenile
looks on and prepares to run.

A large boar munches on a bit of grass and rests his eyes.

A sow gently plays with her yearling cub while fishing.

Like mother, like daughter. Young cubs learn everything their first year.

Red foxes are never far away from the best bear fishing areas because they can quickly cruise the banks and pick up salmon pieces the bears have dropped.

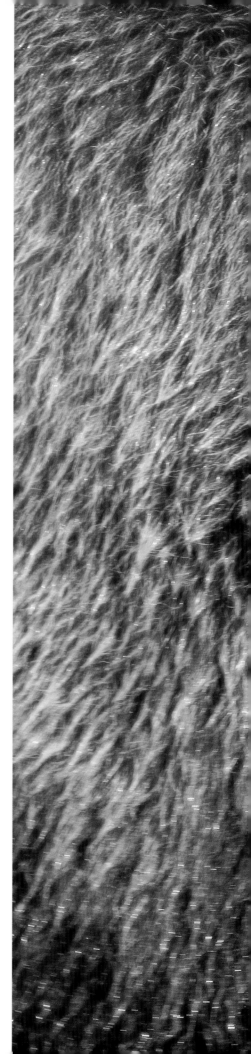

The closest I have ever gotten to a bear giving me the evil eye.

Two of this years sibling cubs take time to wrestle and play near some alder trees.

A tiny cub hams it up for the camera while mom fishes for lunch.

A fairly rare sighting on Kodiak. This sow fishes with her four second year cubs.

This juvenile bear has learned to walk the beach looking for food the tide has washed up.

After an unsuccessful underwater dive,
this sow watches me very closely.

At two years old, this cub experiments with his sleeping style

This juvenile bear was quite afraid of me and hid for a moment behind this small tree before bolting off into the September fireweed.

After catching a shoal spawner, this bear takes his breakfast of sockeye to shore to eat.

A bear picks his way across the waterfall
trying to find lunch along the way.

This young cub has a very chocolate colored coat for
a Kodiak Bear, even with his white collar.

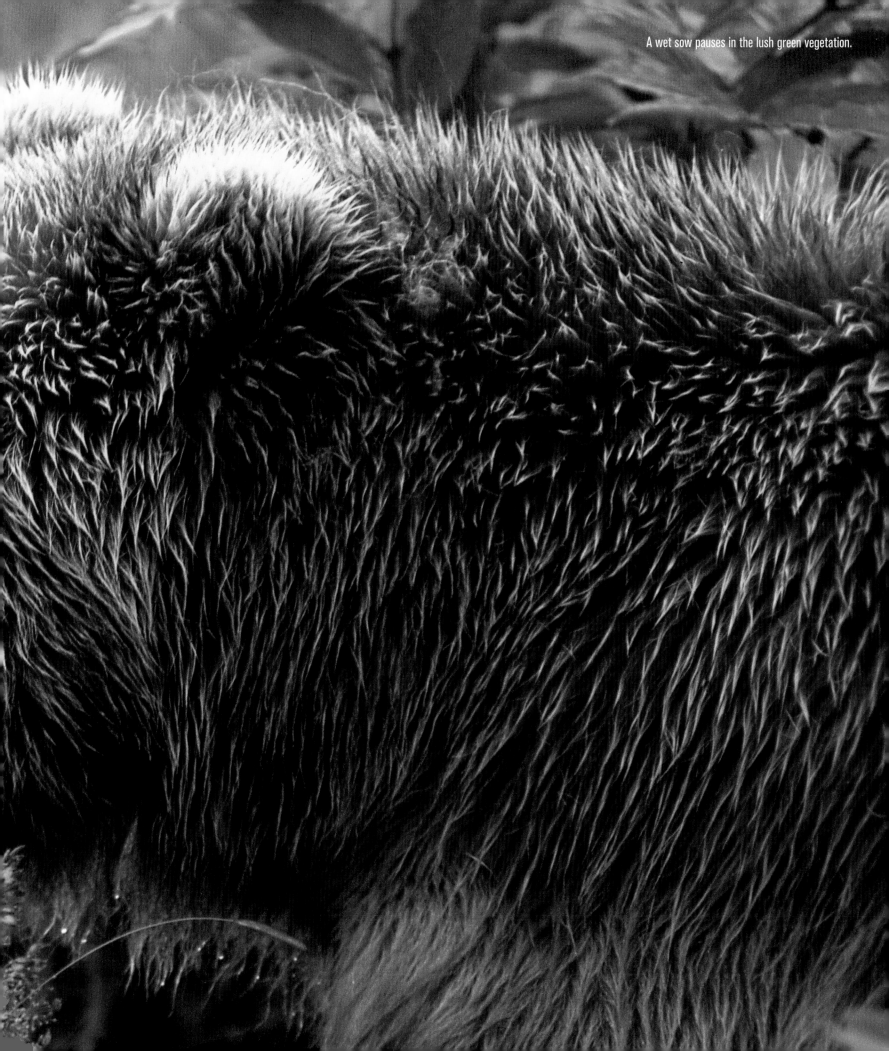

A wet sow pauses in the lush green vegetation.

Water flies as these two bears tussle over a fishing spot.

As he patrolled the river bank, this boar never let me out of his sight.

This tiny cub has to stretch to see what mom sees.

This sow stops for a rest under a stand of alder trees
near a small stream.

This group of Sitka black-tailed deer appeared along the river in an area where two bears had been just ten minutes before.

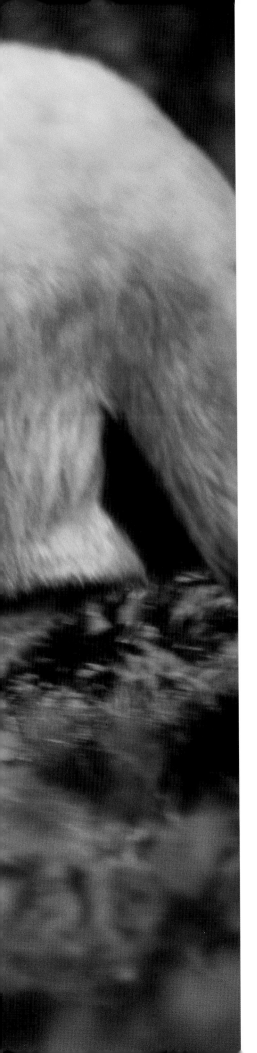

A sow charges through the brush at sunset.

Sometimes fights break out as bears compete
for the best fishing spots.

Being driven from the prime river fishing spots by bigger bears, this juvenile bear has learned to catch some shoal spawning sockeye along the lakeshore.

A break in the clouds at sunrise can create dramatic scenes like this one of the sun on the fall colored peninsula.

This red fox stops for a brief second to check me out before he resumes his beach combing.

This huge mature boar is the biggest bear I have ever photographed. He appeared out of nowhere, walking along the river as all the other bears left the water. As soon as he got downwind of me he disappeared into the brush as quickly as he had appeared, never to be seen again.

Before this bear heads out across the grassy beach, he stops to make sure I don't follow any closer.

This boar bursts through the brush as the sunset glistens on the yellow leaves of fall.

This young cub finds it easier to climb up a tree than to climb down.

Very small cubs like this one have to work to cross even small streams.

Adult boars tend mostly to be nocturnal loners, and are rarely spotted while other bears are around.

This juvenile bear splashes in the water while the sun rises behind him.

This juvenile bear looks around for his competition before he eats
his tail-caught sockeye salmon.

A red fox and a magpie comb the river shallows looking for any
salmon the bears may have left.

Some bears prefer to recline while they eat their salmon.

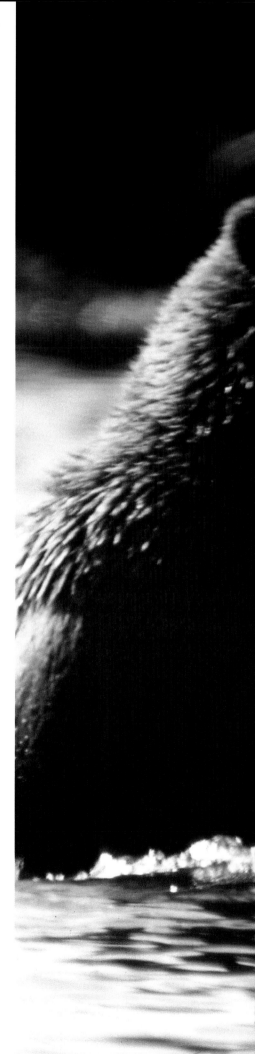

Two juvenile bears spar with each other as they practice for
later dominance tests they will face.

Kodiak Island is a maze of breathtaking mountains and stunning bays

This juvenile bear glistens as he fishes midstream.

The light gold coat of this sow creates a beautiful reflection in the river as she wades in to fish at sunset.

This juvenile bear is not a great fisherman yet, so he is happy
to eat everything he catches, tail and all.

This immature bald eagle rests on the lake shore after eating
some salmon bits left by the bears

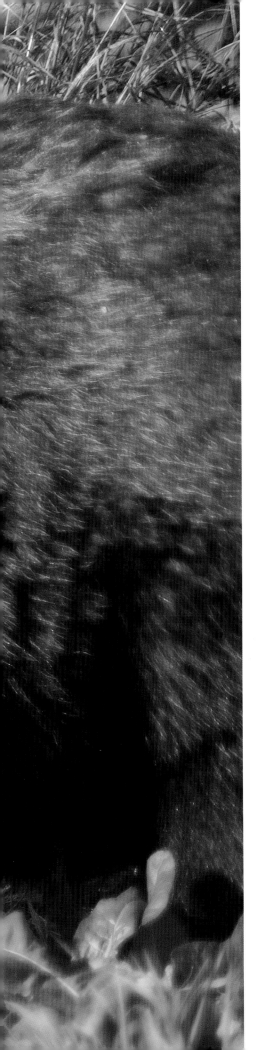

Big boars are distinctive from the other bears by their much rounder and stockier appearance.

Sometimes they seem almost humanlike as they sit and look around.

FROM THE PHOTOGRAPHER

ON MY FIRST TRIP TO ALASKA I FELL IN LOVE NOT ONLY WITH THE SIGHTS AND SOUNDS OF THE ALASKAN WILDERNESS BUT WITH THE TRUE SOLITUDE THAT CAN STILL BE FOUND THERE.

My journey with the bears of Kodiak Island began in the summer of 1999. On my first trip to Alaska I fell in love not only with the sights and sounds of the Alaskan wilderness but with the true solitude that can still be found there. On subsequent trips I found myself drawn deeper and deeper into the world of the Kodiak bear.

Initially, I was taking pictures of all of the animals for use in my stock photography library. I never really thought about a book or even if I would return to visit Kodiak again the next year. Over time a strange thing kept happening to me. When I was at home in Minneapolis on cold January nights I would feel an emptiness in the pit of my stomach that made me dream about Kodiak and the bears. As I made subsequent trips I began to realize that for

First with Dan Dorman of Highline Air and now with Dave Hilty of Bear Quest Aviation this same Cessna 206 has carried me safely around the island many times.

124

Two bears wrestle in front of a typical Kodiak backdrop.

A dense fog rolls in from Katmai across the Shelikof Strait and begins to blanket Kodiak Island.

me, it was about more than getting pictures of the bears. I was drawn to the world in which they roam. The land is rugged and hard with steep mountains and long deep coastal bays. It is beautiful and delicate with fields of pink fireweed and gentle green vegetation. This is a world where Kodiak bears live a wild existence like their ancestors have for some 12,000 years.

This has been more than a book project for me. It has helped to define who I am as a photographer and as a person. As I look back at the images I've captured of these magnificent animals, I can remember each animal and what it was like

A lone bear stops his stroll along the beach to see why I am following him.

I want to say a few words about bear etiquette and safet These are wild animals living in a wilderness settin People need to understand that when we visit, we are th guests in their world. We owe it to the animals and th people who want to see them to take this seriously. Bea viewing has become very popular in Alaska. As a result o this, bears can become socialized to human presence. Yo may even think that they are acting tame, but they are not Please try to remember the deadly consequences for peopl and bears if someone does something foolish.

photographing that day. I remember when the bears seemed bothered by my presence and when they didn't. I remember which bears I looked forward to seeing over and over and which ones I hoped to never see again.

The question I'm asked most frequently about photographing the bears of Kodiak is, "How close do you get to them?" Suffice to say, I don't ever try to creep up on bears. I set up in areas that I know they frequent and wait for them to come to me. With this said, sometimes the bears come closer than I would like, and I've even had to politely ask them to back off a little.

A sow and her cub play along a hillsid

Two bears struggle to maintain their grip upon the hill they are climbing.

The idea of creating this book came to me as I pondered how I could help educate Alaskan tourists as well as animal lovers all over the world about the bears of Kodiak Island. From the beginning I wanted to create a beautiful and meaningful resource for people to learn and admire the bears the way I do. I hope that in some small way this book brings the Kodiak bear into the hearts and minds of new people.

I feel very blessed that I have had the opportunity to explore Kodiak Island and live for brief periods in the world of the Kodiak Kings.

Best regards,

JASON WOOD

ACKNOWLEDGEMENTS

I would like to take a moment to give special thanks to the following people without whose help this project would not have been possible.

Thanks to…

Reneé Wood, *for your inspiring example and your many encouraging words.*

Sarah Ward Rathe, *for your beautiful design work.*

Norton Stillman, *for all of your advice and expertise in publishing.*

Judy Olausen, *for all of your encouragement and introducing me to Norton.*

Jason Rathe, *for daring to go where no man has gone before, even after the earthquake.*

Dan Stevens, *for floating the Chilikadrotna with me, even if it didn't make it in this book.*

Bryce Christopherson, *for two glorious weeks: one tent bound, one sunshine.*

Jamie Swick, *for sharing a trip of a lifetime paddling through salmon and watching ocean sunsets.*

Brian Wood, *for helping me explore and guide and catch a few fish in-between.*

Dan Dorman & Kim Petersen, *for getting me started with location ideas and flying me around Kodiak safely.*

Dave Hilty & Heather Johnson, *for being so helpful in flying me around Kodiak safely.*

Jim Hamilton, *for believing that photography is important to bear viewers.*

Kodiak National Wildlife Refuge, *for allowing me to photograph in the refuge.*

Koniag Native Corporation, *for allowing me to photograph on native land.*

Sean & Jen Petersen, *for letting me stay at your places and use your car so many times.*

Heidi Kopacek, *for letting me stay at your house and driving all over Alaska to pick me up.*

Floyd & Carolyn Tanner, *for letting me stay so many times at the Ho-Hum Lodge in Seward.*

Thomas Wood, *for giving me the spirit of outdoor adventure.*

Sandee Wood, *for bringing me into this beautiful world and letting me see it.*

Gretchen Johnson, *for all of your help in looking for publishers.*

Jim Gallop, *for the 400 f/2.8 you sold me – it is still sharper than ever.*

Larry Van Daele, *for writing a thoughtful and informative introduction worthy of these great bears.*

And to all of the other wonderful people that my limited memory has left off this list.